Berlitz ®

Italian

Little Simon

LITTLE SIMON
An imprint of Simon & Schuster Children's Publishing Division
1230 Avenue of the Americas
New York, New York 10020

LITTLE SIMON and colophon are registered trademarks of Simon & Schuster.

Printed in USA

10   9   8   7   6   5   4   3

Library of Congress Cataloging-in-Publication Data

Berlitz Jr. Italian.–1st Aladdin Books ed.
p.   cm.
English and Italian.

Summary: A conversation and phrase book for learning simple Italian.
ISBN 0-689-71593-5 (book).

1. Italian language–Conversation and phrase books–English–Juvenile literature. [1. Italian
language–Conversation and phrase books.] 1. Berlitz Schools of Languages of America.
PC1121.B465   1992
458.3'421—dc20   91-21143

To the parent:

Learning a foreign language is one of the best ways to expand a child's horizons. It immediately exposes him or her to a foreign culture—especially important in a time when the world is more of a "global village" than ever before.

Berlitz Jr. is the first Berlitz program of its kind. Like the adult language programs that Berlitz pioneered, the Berlitz Jr. teaching method is based on clear and simplified conversations, without the need for grammatical drills. Within minutes, just by listening to our sixty-minute cassette and following the beautifully illustrated text, your child will be saying a few simple but invaluable foreign phrases.

Your child will love Teddy and enjoy meeting his family and friends. Together you and your child can follow Teddy to school, where he learns how to count and spell, and then on to playtime in the park and a visit to the circus. All you have to do is listen and repeat. You will hear native speakers saying each phrase clearly. There is a long pause after each phrase so that your child can repeat it, imitating the authentic pronunciation. Music and sound effects add to the fun.

All the phrases on the cassette are found in the book, together with a translation, illustrated by lively and appealing drawings. And if you want to find the exact meaning of a word quickly, just look it up in the foreign-language vocabulary at the back of the book. The book and cassette reinforce each other but can be used separately once your child is comfortable with them.

All children have the potential to speak a foreign language. By using frequently repeated words in a storybook form, Teddy Berlitz allows children to tap that potential. These carefully constructed texts have been approved by school language-experts and meet the Berlitz standard of quality. Best of all, the book-cassette format enables a new language to be learned in much the same way your child first learned to speak.

Enjoy sharing Teddy Berlitz—and watching your child's world grow.

Berlitz Publishing

Ecco Teddy!
Here's Teddy!

Ciao! Mi chiamo Teddy.
Hello! My name is Teddy.

Io sono un orso.
I am a bear.

Io parlo italiano.
I speak Italian.

E tu, parli italiano?
And you? Do you speak Italian?

Sì.
Yes.

No.
No.

No, non parlo italiano.
No, I don't speak Italian.

Parli inglese?
Do you speak English?

Sì.
Yes.

No.
No.

Sì, parlo inglese.
Yes, I speak English.

Mi chiamo Teddy.
My name is Teddy.

E tu, come ti chiami?
And you? What's your name?

Scusa? Come ti chiami?
Excuse me? What's your name?

Mi chiamo....
My name is....

Grazie!
Thank you!

Questa è casa mia.
This is my house.

La mia casa è nel bosco.
My house is in the forest.

La mia casa è piccola. Non è grande.
My house is little. It isn't big.

Ci sono molti alberi e fiori nel bosco.
There are many trees and flowers in the forest.

E' un bel bosco.
It's a beautiful forest.

Questo è il mio papà.
This is my daddy.

Questa è la mia mamma.
This is my mommy.

Voglio bene al mio papà.
I love my daddy.

Voglio bene alla mia mamma.
I love my mommy.

Voglio bene ai miei genitori.
I love my parents.

I miei genitori dicono "ciao."
My parents say "hello."

Ho una sorella.
I have a sister.

Ho un fratello.
I have a brother.

Mio fratello si chiama Paolo.
My brother's name is Paolo.

Mia sorella si chiama Lucia.
My sister's name is Lucia.

Io sono grande.
I am big.

Paolo e Lucia sono piccoli.
Paolo and Lucia are little.

Sono bambini!
They are babies!

Abbiamo molti giocattoli.
We have lots of toys.

Abbiamo:
We have:

un treno
a train

una palla
a ball

una bambola
a doll

una macchina
a car

un aereo
a plane

una barca
a boat

un secchiello ed una paletta.
a pail and a shovel.

Ci piace molto giocare.
We really like to play.

Questa è la mia scuola.
This is my school.

La mia scuola è in città.
My school is in the town.

1 LUNEDÌ

2 MARTEDÌ

3 MERCOLEDÌ

4 GIOVEDÌ

5 VENERDÌ

Vado a scuola il lunedì, il martedì,
il mercoledì, il giovedì, e il venerdì.
I go to school on Monday, Tuesday, Wednesday,
Thursday, and Friday.

6 SABATO

7 DOMENICA

Non vado a scuola il sabato e la domenica.
I don't go to school on Saturday and Sunday.

Oggi è lunedì. Vado a scuola.
Today is Monday. I am going to school.

Questa è la mia classe.
This is my classroom.

Questa è la mia maestra.
This is my teacher.

Buon giorno, sono la signora Rossi.
Good morning, I am Mrs. Rossi.

Saluta la signora Rossi.
Say hello to Mrs. Rossi.

Buon giorno.
Hello.

Questa è Gina.
This is Gina.

Ciao.
Hi.

Gina è la maestra?
Is Gina the teacher?

No, non è la maestra.
No, she is not the teacher.

Gina non è la Signora Rossi.
Gina is not Mrs. Rossi.

Gina è un' allieva!
Gina is a student!

Gina legge i numeri.
Gina is reading the numbers.

Uno, due, tre, quattro, cinque, sei, sette, otto, nove, dieci.
One, two, three, four, five, six, seven, eight, nine, ten.

Contiamo da uno a dieci.
Let's count from one to ten.

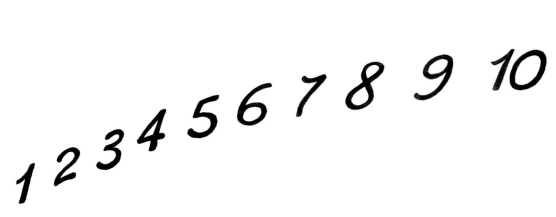

Puoi contare con Gina?
Can you count with Gina?

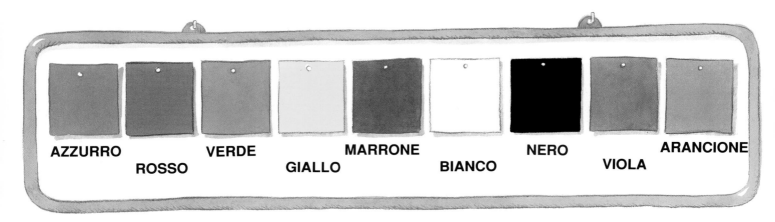

AZZURRO ROSSO VERDE GIALLO MARRONE BIANCO NERO VIOLA ARANCIONE

Ecco Mario.
This is Mario.

Mario gioca con i colori.
Mario is playing with the colors.

Azzurro, rosso, verde, giallo, marrone, bianco, nero, viola, arancione.
Blue, red, green, yellow, brown, white, black, violet, orange.

Sai scrivere?
Do you know how to write?

Scrivo A, B, C....
I'm writing A, B, C....

Guarda! Scrivo l'alfabeto: A, B, C, D, E....
Look! I'm writing the alphabet: A, B, C, D, E....

Adesso leggo l'alfabeto:
Now I'm reading the alphabet:

A,B,C,D,E,F,G,H,I,J,K,L,M,N,O,P,Q,R,S,T,U,V,W,X,Y,Z.

Teddy, sai scrivere il tuo nome?
Teddy, do you know how to write your name?

Teddy! Sono io.
Teddy! That's me.

E tu? Sai scrivere il tuo nome?
And you? Can you write your name?

Cantiamo a scuola.
We sing at school.

Ecco una canzone.
Here's a song.

E tu? Che cosa ci canti?
And you? Will you sing with us?

Dai, canta con noi!
Come on, sing with us!

Uno...due...tre
One...two...three

Fra Martino, campanaro
Dormi tu, dormi tu?
Suona le campane,
  suona le campane!
Ding dong dang,
Ding dong dang

Brother Martin, bell ringer
Are you sleeping? Are you sleeping?
Morning bells are ringing,
Morning bells are ringing,
Ding, dong, dang
ding, dong, dang

Bene! Molto bene!
Good! Very good!

Che ore sono?
What time is it?

Sono le tre!
It's three o'clock!

E' l'una? No.
Is it one o'clock? No.

Sono le due?
Is it two o'clock?

No. Sono le tre. Evviva!
No. It's three o'clock. Yaay!

La scuola è finita.
School is over.

Arrivederci, signora Rossi!
Good-bye, Mrs. Rossi!

SCUOLA

Ciao, Teddy!
Good-bye, Teddy!

Ciao, Gina!
Good-bye, Gina!

Ciao, Mario!
Good-bye, Mario!

La Sorpresa
The Surprise

Andiamo al parco giochi.
Let's go to the playground.

Il parco giochi è vicino alla scuola.
The playground is near the school.

Ci sono molte cose da fare nel parco giochi.
There are a lot of things to do in the playground.

Andiamo tutti sulla giostra.
Let's all go on the merry-go-round.

Sono sull'altalena!
I'm on the swing!

Scendo dallo scivolo.
I'm going down the slide.

Alle quattro andiamo tutti a casa.

At four o'clock we all go home.

Cammino verso il bosco.
I walk to the forest.

Cammino sulla strada.
I walk on the road.

C'e un manifesto sull'albero.
There is a poster on a tree.
Sul manifesto leggo: "Circo."
On the poster I read: "Circus."

Che divertimento!
That's fun!

E quando torno a casa - sorpresa!
And when I get home - surprise!

Teddy, vuoi andare al circo?
Teddy, do you want to go to the circus?

Al circo? Sí! Andiamo!
To the circus? Yes! Let's go!

CIRCO

Sabato la mamma mi porta al circo.
On Saturday Mommy takes me to the circus.

Paolo e Lucia rimangono a casa con papà.
Paolo and Lucia stay at home with Daddy.

Il circo è vicino al parco.
The circus is near the park.

La tenda del circo è rossa e azzurra.
The circus tent is red and blue.

C' è molta gente in fila.
There are many people in line.

Ciao, mi chiamo Giulia.
Hi, my name is Giulia.

Ciao, sono Teddy.
Hi, I'm Teddy.

Questo è mio fratello Fabio.
This is my brother Fabio.

Sediamoci insieme.
Let's all sit together.

Ci sono dei coccodrilli nel circo?
Are there crocodiles in the circus?

No, ma ci sono dei leoni.
No, but there are lions.

Ci sono delle giraffe nel circo?
Are there giraffes in the circus?

No, ma ci sono delle zebre.
No, but there are zebras.

Ci sono anche delle scimmie.
There are monkeys, too.

Quante scimmie ci sono?
How many monkeys?

Non lo so. Contiamole: una, due,
I don't know. Let's count them: one, two,
tre, quattro, cinque, sei. Sei scimmie.
three, four, five, six. Six monkeys.

Ecco un elefante. Quanto è grande!
Here's an elephant. How big he is!

Guarda, due pagliacci!
Look, two clowns!

Uno è allegro, l'altro è triste.
One is happy, the other is sad.

Ecco la parata! E'grande!
Here's the parade! It's a big parade!

Guarda tutti gli animali!
Look at all the animals!

Dopo il circo, compriamo un gelato.
After the circus, we buy ice cream.

Voglio il gelato al cioccolato.
I want chocolate ice cream.

Voglio il gelato alla fragola.
I want strawberry ice cream.

Lo voglio alla vaniglia.
I'll have vanilla.

Fabio, dove abiti?
Fabio, where do you live?

Abito vicino al parco giochi.
I live near the playground.

Vai a scuola qui vicino?
Do you go to school near here?

Sì.
Yes.

Bene, possiamo giocare insieme dopo scuola.
Good, we can play together after school.

Ciao, Fabio.
Good-bye, Fabio.

Ciao, Teddy.
Good-bye, Teddy.

Vocabulary

A

a – to, at

    a casa – at home (with a)

abitare – to live

adesso – now

aereo – plane

al (a+il) – to the

albero, alberi – tree, trees

alfabeto – alphabet

alle quattro – at four o'clock

allegro – happy

allievo, allieva – student

altalena – swing

amico – friend

anche – too

andare – to go

    Andiamo! – Let's go!

    Vado – (I) go,

    Vado a scuola – (I) go to school,

    Vado al parco giochi – (I'm) going to the playground.

    Vai a scuola lì? – Do you go to school there?

animale – animal

arancione – orange

arrivederci – good-bye

automobile – car

avere – to have

    abbiamo-(we) have

ho – (I) have

azzurro – blue

B

bambino, bambini – baby, babies/child, children

bambola – doll

barca – boat

bello, bella – beautiful

bene! – good!

bianco – white

bosco – forest

buon giorno – good morning

C

calmarsi – to be quiet.

    Calmatevi ragazzi. – Be quiet, children.

camminare – to walk

    Cammino verso casa. – I'm walking home.

campane – bells

cantare – to sing

    Cantiamo a scuola. – We sing at school.

Cantiamo una canzone! – Let's sing a song!

canzone – song

casa – house

Che cosa è? – What is it?

Che divertimento! – What fun!

Che ore sono? – What time is it?

chiamarsi – to be called

Si chiama Paolo. – His name is Paolo.

ci – us, we

Ci piace giocare. – We like to play.

ci sono – there are

Ci sono dei leoni? – Are there any lions?

Ci sono sei scimmie. – There are six monkeys.

ciao – hi, hello

cinque – five

cioccolato – chocolate

circo – circus

città – city, town

classe – classroom

coccodrillo – crocodile

colori – colors

Come ti chiami? – What's your name?

comprare – to buy

Compriamo un gelato. – We buy an ice cream.

contare – to count

Contiamole! – Let's count them!

Contiamo! – Let's count!

cosa, cose – thing, things

D

da – from

Dai! – Come on!

da...a – from...to

del, della, dei, delle – some, any

dieci – ten

dire – to say

Dice "Circo." – (It) says Circus.

Dicono – (They) say.

domenica – Sunday

dopo – after

dormire – to sleep

Dormi? – Are you sleeping?

dove? – where?

Dove abiti? – Where do you live?

Dove vai? – Where are you going?

due – two

E

ecco – here is, here are

Ecco il mio amico Mario. – Here is my friend Mario.

elefante – elephant

essere – to be

è – he, she, it is

É l'una? – Is it one o'clock?

sono – (I) am, (they) are

F

fare – to do

fila – line

C'è molta gente in fila. – There are many people in line.

finito, finita – finished

fiore, fiori – flower, flowers

fra – brother

fra Martino – brother Martin

fragola – strawberry

fratello – brother

G

gelato – ice cream

gelato al cioccolato – chocolate ice cream

genitori – parents

gente – people

giallo – yellow

Gina è un'allieva. – Gina is a student.

Gina legge i numeri. – Gina is reading the numbers.

Giocare – to play

Mario giocare con i colori. – Mario is playing with the colors.

giocattolo, giocattoli – toy, toys

giostra – merry-go-round

giovedi – Thursday

giraffa – giraffe

grande, grandi – big

grazie – thank you, thanks

guardare – to look

guarda! – to look!

Guarda tutti gli animali! – Look at all the animals!

I

il – the
> **Il Circo è vicino.** – The Circus is near.

in – in

inglese – English

insieme – together

io – I

italiano – Italian

L

la – the
> **La mia casa è piccola.** – My house is small.
>
> **La scuola è finita.** – School is finished.

leggere – to read

leone – lion

lì – there

Lucia e Paolo sono piccoli. – Lucia and Paolo are small.

lunedì – Monday

l'altro – the other
> **L'altro è allegro.** – The other one is happy.

M

maestra – teacher

mamma – mommy
> **La mamma mi porta al Circo.** – Mommy takes me to the Circus.

manifesto – poster

marrone – brown

martedì – Tuesday

mercoledì – Wednesday

mi – me
> **Mi chiamo Teddy.** – My name is Teddy.

mio, mia, miei, mie – my

molto, molti, molta, molte – many
> **molta gente** – many people
>
> **molte cose** – many things
>
> **molti alberi** – many trees

N

nel (in+il) – in the
> **nel parco giochi** – in the playground

nero – black

no – no

non lo so – (I) don't know (it)

non parlo italiano – (I) don't speak Italian

nove – nine

O

oggi – today

ora – now

orso – bear

otto – eight

P

pagliaccio – clown

paletta – spade

palla – ball

papà – daddy

parco giochi – playground

parlare – to speak
> **Parli italiano?** – Do you speak Italian?
>
> **Parlo** – (I) speak,

piacere – to like

piccolo, piccola, piccoli, piccole – small

pista – circus ring

portare – to take, to bring

potere – to be able
> **possiamo giocare** – (we) can play

Q

quando – when
> **quando torno a casa** – when I get home

quanto – how much

quanti – how many
> **Quante scimmie a sono?** – How many monkeys are there?

quattro – four

questo, questa, questi, queste – this
> **questo è** – this is
>
> **Questa è la mia casa.** – This is my house.

R

rimanere – to stay
> **Rimangono a casa** – (They) stay at home.

rosso – red

S

sabato – Saturday
salutare – to say hello
    Saluta le mia maestra! – Say hello to my teacher!
sapere – to know, to be able to
    Sai contare? – Can you count?
    Sai contare da 1 a 10? – Can you count from 1 to 10?
    Sai fare molte cose. – You can do many things.
    Sai scrivere il tuo nome? – Can you write your name?
    so scrivere – (I) know how to write.
scendere – to go down
    scendo dallo scivolo – (I'm) going down the slide.
scimmia – monkey
scivolo – slide
scrivere – to write
    scrivo – (I) write
scuola – school
scusa – sorry, pardon
secchiello – bucket
sedersi – to sit down
    Sediamoci! – Let's sit down.
sei – six
sette – seven
signora – Mrs.
sì – yes
sono – (I) am, (they) are
    Sono bambini. – They are babies.
    Sono io! – That's me.
    Sono le due? – Is it two o'clock?
    Sono le tre – It's three o'clock.
    Sono le tre? – Is it three o'clock?
    Sono sull'altalena. – (I am) on the swing.
sorella – sister
sorpresa – surprise
stare – to be, to stay
    sto a casa – (I) stay at home.
strada – road
    sulla strada – on the road
suonare – to ring
    suona – ring!
    Suona le campane! – Ring the bells!

T

tenda – tent
te – you
tornare – to return, to get back
tre – three
treno – train
triste – sad
tu – you
tuo – your
tutti – everyone, all
    Tutti sono in pista. – Everyone is in the ring.

U

uno – one

V

vaniglia – vanilla
vedere – to see
    Vedo un manifesto – (I) see a poster.
venerdi – Friday
verde – green
verso – to, toward
    verso il bosco – to the forest
vicino a – near
viola – violet
volere – to want
    voglio – (I) want
    Vuoi andare al Circo? – Do you want to go to the circus?
    Vuoi cantare con noi? – Do you want to sing with us?
volere bene a... – to love
    Voglio bene ai miei genitori. – I love my parents.
    Voglio bene al mio papà. – I love my daddy.
    Voglio bene alla mia mamma. – I love my mommy.

Z

zebra – zebra